Text: Cambria
Design: One Thought, Inc.
Photos and artwork: One Thought, Inc. and Tochi Brown.
Cover illustration: Courtesy of CreateSpace
Author photo: © Tochi Brown Adimiche

I0164110

Some of the chapters have been previously published online on tochi.us and Facebook.com in slightly different editions.

Library of Congress Cataloging-in-Publication Data
Stand! When There's Nothing Else You Can Do Right Now
        by Tochi Brown

ISBN 978-097-60659-6-8 (Paperback)

1. Creative writing. 2. English language-Rhetoric. 3. Self-help. 4. Spirituality.

An Imprint of One Thought Press
P O Box 130938, The Woodlands, TX 77393, USA
http:// onethought.us

✖

To all who are acutely, chronically or occasionally, at their wits' end
– despite all their honest efforts –
this is for you.

⌘

Table of Contents

✄

Introduction

This world can be a tough place, even for those whom we think 'have it all'. The daily media has no short supply of stories about misfortunes and sundry worries that beset both the rich and poor alike. Many are without guidance, without a clue, without that glimmer of light that will enable them to find their own way out of their difficulties. That is a tragedy in itself. Others have false, incomplete or inappropriate counsel, which causes them to dig deeper into the morass in which they already find themselves, worsening their already sad situation.

Therefore, the reason why there are millions – if not billions – of self help materials out there by millions of authors is that no one method, perspective or approach of inspiration appeals to *everyone*. Besides, there are billions of people who have little or no access to these materials; if and when they eventually do, they will be sure to find something that perfectly addresses their situation.

I'm no different from anyone else in needing constant boosters to my morale and psyche. When I'm mentally and spiritually exhausted to keep my own head above water, I look to words of wisdom from someone else to buoy me in place till I regain my strength. Granted that what they say may be trite or something I already know, but there is something about hearing Truth expressed by someone else, sometimes in a simple or unique way, which gingers the mind to pick up its own lifeward rhythm. That which I read or hear is the reminder to me that no condition is permanent, for "This, too, shall pass!" Therefore, I must remain peaceful, inwardly silent, strong – and courageous.

Courage – this is the ultimate theme of this book. We must learn how to be courageous in the face of every adversity that will (not *may*) beset us. Whether the adversity is of our own making, or from another, the same mindset must apply. Be courageous. Fear nothing, no matter how it manifests. Concern yourself with no public opinion or condemnation – that is none of your business. You may be delayed, detoured or (temporarily) deceived, but choose not to be denied.

I understand and accept that this book is not for everyone. It was not intended to be. Instead, I have written it for my encouragement, and for everyone else out there who just needs some plain, uncomplicated talk right now. For people just like me, I hope and pray that this little book will do for you what it has done for me in the writing of it – that it toughens you mentally and spiritually till you emerge victorious on the other side of whatever dilemma, difficulty or distress you are encountering right now.

Stand fast, dear one, until the break of dawn. Fear nothing!

Tochi Brown
Lagos, Nigeria.

✄

The Dominant Voice Versus the Authentic Voice

Many of us are confused by the voices we hear, truly believing that the loudest one is our own. But when the instructions of that dominant voice fails to bring us the relief we seek, we are forced to ask – *Is this voice really mine? Am I the one speaking? Have I said this before? Or did I hear this from someone else?*

We all are in this marketplace called life. We are all sellers. We are all buyers. Some sellers are louder and more aggressive than others. Some buyers are more gullible than others. Regardless of who is buying and who is selling, *we are solely responsible for what we buy in the marketplace. We assume all risks and all benefits when we choose from whom we will buy.* It's the dominant, discouraging voices coming out of us and running around in our heads that we have to silence first, in order to hear our real self speak.

At the end of the day, from whom do we buy? How do we know which ideas are the safest to follow? By recognizing and listening to our own authentic voice, and taking immediate action on the truth as spoken by our own authentic voice.

Here are some clues as to whether we are hearing from our authentic self, or from a dominant voice inside our heads:

1. The dominant voice:
    - Tells you to do what you know is wrong;
    - Lies to you about your situation in order to influence your decision, and you know it;
    - Tells you change yourself just to fit in or be accepted by others;
    - Tells you to take certain actions based on what others might think or say of you;
    - Calls you bad names if you don't do what it tells you to do;
    - Constantly condemns and negatively criticizes you;
    - Makes you lose your self-confidence and courage;
    - Makes you fearful of the consequences if you should take action on your own behalf.
2. Our authentic voice:
    - Tells you the truth of every situation, so that you can make your own decision;
    - Emboldens you to defend yourself;
    - Encourages you to stand before anyone;
    - Increases the feeling of freedom in your mind and body;
    - Relieves you or another of suffering or pain;
    - Saves your live, or the life of another;
    - Maintains or increases your dignity, self-respect and confidence;
    - Makes things flow and work out well in your life.

Understand this: Many people around you are struggling with this same issue. They are unable – or unwilling – to differentiate between the dominant and authentic voices they hear. Don't be dismayed or upset about this! That is why they make mistakes like you, and are unable to offer you the genuine and appropriate counsel you need at this time. That's why it is imperative that you determine your authentic voice for yourself. You will make mistakes, but the more you practice, the better you'll get. Remember, your life depends on it.

⌘

At this time, be reminded that you and I are responsible for our own encouragement. No other voice will cheer us on louder than our own. It is up to you and I to remind ourselves that we are *The Tiger, The Victor, The Vanquisher, The Overcomer*, and that the <u>only</u> option we have is to win.

Take responsibility for encouraging yourself, for cheering yourself on, for seeing your way clear, for making it through. After the initial sympathies and kind comments about your situation, people will quickly revert to their preoccupation with their personal concerns... or a growing dread of hearing more about yours.

Just as importantly, we must learn to actively quell the mental storm that daily goes on inside our heads. A great deal of this commotion ensues when we compare ourselves with others. We become negative (dissatisfied, angry, envious, ashamed, embarrassed, hurt, uncomfortable, fearful) when we look at what others have (intelligence, skills, talents, looks, size, weight, clothes, homes, material things, money, status, jobs, businesses, connections, friends, achievements, awards, accolades, family, children, and so forth) and compare them with what we do not have. We have to remind ourselves is that as all fingers on one hand are not equal, so it is with us humans. We must remember to compare ourselves with no one else but our own selves. This is not to say that we must not strive to gain what we want, but to escape the mental turmoil that comes from the untenable and unending race of acquisition to be better than the next person.

It was hard for me growing up and seeing other kids having what I didn't have, or what I wanted to have. What made it worse for me was that it wasn't even about extras or luxury items: what I wanted, I actually needed. Over the years, I learned how to compare myself unfavorably with others, to confirm how much more of a victim of life circumstances I was. But this kind of thinking never motivated me to improve my situation. In fact, my mental state worsened whenever someone pushed the buttons of my 'deficiencies'. I went back to feeling sorry for myself, accepting that I would never measure up, never meet up, never be worthy enough.

But thank goodness, all of that changed when I came in contact with life-affirming people and self-development materials. I had to take responsibility for the cheerleading – or lack thereof – going on inside my head. I had to force myself to flip the script, become aggressive about the health of my soul and choose to experience my life through my own lenses. Regardless of the labels others put on me, I chose the labels I wanted for myself. I had to rename myself, inside and out... and what a change that wrought in my life!

Speak to yourself words of encouragement and power. Tell yourself what you wish others would tell you. On some days, being courageous consists of doing nothing but just talking yourself out of quitting when all about you is despair, desolation, discouragement and disappointment.

Keep talking. Tell yourself what you need to hear. It happens to <u>everyone.</u>

Understand this: Continue speaking until you get what you want or better. It's not over – until you say so. Practicing this mindset is one way we can remain at peace with ourselves regardless of what is going on 'out there'.

✄

I got a call from one of my friends in another state. Basically, the gist was that I had done 'something' to look the way I do now. "Something like what?" I innocently inquired. Within minutes, the conversation degenerated into lurid details of what people 'out there' had said about me, rumors of my lifestyle, speculations about my relationships, what my significant other did for a living, who was in related to me, my kind of friends, the extent of my skills, what my 'correct' body size should be, the amount of my possessions (or lack thereof), the program I should have studied in college, why I wasn't like other women and so on.

My eyes got bigger by the minute. My eyebrows kept rising to meet my hairline. My open mouth got wider. My toes were curled. My ears started to burn. I had no idea anyone was that interested in me. Being a pretty private person, I was mortified. How did all these stories start? And *who were these people anyway*?

But somewhere in the midst of my physiological reactions, I had to force myself to stop reacting and start reinforcing my mind:

- What did I know about myself?
- What did I believe about myself?
- What did I envision for myself?
- Whose opinions were the most important to me?

Mine! My opinions about myself superseded everyone else's!

Understand this: Other people's opinions of you and I are just that – opinions. Opinions are not immutable physical or spiritual laws. Everybody has an opinion on something. When you are going about the business of your life, teach yourself to stop getting derailed by other people's opinions about you, what you do or where you are. Make their opinions none of your business, so that you can focus on what truly is your business.

❈

I have an adult nephew who is a great storyteller. He lived for several years with another well-to-do cousin, for free. Apparently, he knows a great deal about current affairs, historical facts, family relationships and traditional customs. Also, he is a professional victim. Every chance he gets, he tells of the unimaginable obstacles he's had to go through, that he's going through… and yet to go through. To crown it all, he would add that *no one* wanted to help him despite his helpfulness, honesty and loyalty. I used to take him seriously. Based on his complaints, I took time out of my busy schedule to create for him a professional resume. I introduced him to people. I talked to him about the self-respect that comes from independent living. I spent good time with him, encouraging, motivating, guiding, correcting… and *advising*.

Then I went away for four months. After about a month of being away, I stopped hearing from him. No response to my phone calls, emails and text messages. Nothing. When I got back, he was still living with the same cousin, in the 'helpless' situation I originally found him in. I couldn't believe it. Shortly thereafter, a during a conflict, there was a revelation by the cousin that the same nephew had been given financial assistance in the millions – yes, *millions in cash* – but had nothing to show for it.

I, just like millions of others, have come to learn that very many who seek advice really do not want to hear it. They only want to talk and, more often than not, they want to hear themselves talking. This act of talking, in itself, does not have to be considered a terrible thing, for many an intelligent person comes to realize the solution to the vexing problem upon its aural articulation and repetition. Some even reach a definite decision or gain a powerful insight when they hear another voice ask a question about the issue at hand.

Then, what to do about the advice-seekers who really do **not** want a solution? Those for whom asking for counsel is just a procrastination tactic or refusal to accept responsibility for their actions? Those who make us rearrange our schedules to accommodate them at short notice, yet who do not follow through on what we have sincerely advised them to do to solve their problems? Those who shut us down and make us the enemy for doing the very thing they asked us to do?

When we find an inveterate attention-seeker on our hands, it might be best to remain in non-participatory silence so as to conserve our energies for the manifestation of good somewhere else. This kind of silence seeks neither to illustrate nor to punish; rather, it is the buffer that our minds need to prevent circuit overload. This kind of silence helps us avoid needless emotional arousing.

Whatever we focus on, such as the solution to (other people's) problems, consumes our mental energy. Since our mental energy directs and controls our physical energy, that is why we often experience physical tiredness after interacting with chronic advice-seekers. Avoid these energy vampires, those who have no real need for your counsel, who have demonstrated that they are out just to talk *ad nauseam* without taking any real action on their own behalf.

Understand this: Why waste your time speaking to ears that refuse to listen to you? Why waste your time sending love to hearts of stone? Who determined it your duty to be the team player, the peacemaker… the fool? Instead, employ your mental energy wisely and productively, helping those who really need your help. You will be energized by the returned enthusiasm of those who really seek and need solutions.

✼

What makes some people so mentally strong, apparently impervious to the hailstones hurled at them by life? In isolation or in the midst of battle, they remain focused and determined. Speaking to them of things that are contrary to their firm beliefs is a waste of time and energy. These are the ones, rightly or wrongly, who have decided to reside in their own minds.

What does this mean? Our true home is in our consciousness, in our minds. It is true that home is where you make it, and how you make it. It can be as grandiose or as humble as you desire. It is your stronghold, your castle, your fortress, your world, your universe.

Our consciousness is our primary teacher in this life. It is from here that the answers we seek manifest, as long as it is in this direction – inward – that we look. As such, being open-minded and attentive are imperative... open-minded to the opportunity to make a connection; attentive to the counsel that will be given. The counsel must be sought in order for it to be given. There must be a student before there can be a master.

The easiest way to wash out a soapy bottle is to keep filling it with fresh water until all the soapy water is removed from the bottle. Therefore, just as the contents of a container is gradually yet completely changed by the continuous addition of new content, so are the current thoughts and realities of our minds gradually and inevitably replaced by new thoughts and realities that emerge from the deep well of our own consciousness.

Understand this: it is imperative that from time to time, regularly and faithfully, we visit our own mental home for reinforcement, replenishment, renewal and restoration. This way we remain in balance, and quickly bound back from all the sticky stuff that life throws at us.

❈

Occasionally, I struggle with asking for help, but not to the degree that brought me discomfort in the past. What changed? The realization that I needed other people to succeed, and that I had to open my mouth to ask for the help that I needed. I had to overcome my own mental hurdle that it was humiliating to have someone refuse to help me, that everyone would find out, and that I would bear the stigma of rejection for life. Asking for help didn't make me any less intelligent or less worthy to be alive on this planet. So what if the person I asked said "No"? I asked someone else. That's what other human beings were doing and succeeding – and I didn't think any more or less of them either! Furthermore, I came to learn, via various channels, that people were more consumed with their own problems than mine.

Do not concern yourself with those who argue with you or laugh at your efforts to use spirituality, philosophy, psychology or any other method to solve your problems, for she who wears the shoes knows where it hurts. Maybe such persons (may pretend to) have no problems in their lives, or have the facility to ignore their problems, or yet still, have someone else solve their problems for them, hence their easy ridicule of you and yours. Your task, if I may be so bold to remind you, is to achieve your solution to your problem. Not to focus on *why* others do not have the same problem, but *how* they get around the same problem. Then use that knowledge to help yourself.

So, you ask, how do I solve the same or similar problems, such as mine?

1. Ask questions. Ask all the questions you want. This is not the time to be shy or proud, else your problem will eat you up alive. You don't want that.
2. Do your research. Take the time to go online, read literature or watch programs related to your problem and its solution(s).
3. Avoid long debates and pointless analyses of your problem with others. Often times, they can't help you, otherwise, they would have done so and saved you the energy. Again, ignore those who laugh or scoff at you as you seek answers. Later on, they will return to praise you and your success.
4. Be open-minded and receptive. The solution to your problem may come in totally unexpected ways or from unexpected sources. You don't know everything.
5. Take heart. Be courageous. Be willing to do what you haven't done before in order to get the solutions you've never had. Throw overboard *all* outmoded thinking and practices that have not helped you solve your problem. Dive onto the ocean of endless possibilities. Swim for your life.
6. Learn how to generate multiple solutions to problems, no matter how farfetched your 'solutions' may initially appear. Over time, you'll become expert at generating workable solutions for all of your problems.
7. Choose to deal with your challenges, once and for all! Ask yourself: "What is the worst that can possibly happen now?" "Then what?" "No matter what happens, I shall handle it!" So this is what you *must* do: Decide, no matter what, to "fearlessly intercept the challenge", no matter what the challenge may be – relationship, situation, person, or thing.

When you deal with the tough tribulations you encounter in life with evasion, avoidance, detours and indirectness, do not think for one moment that you have been tempered enough to handle those hard problems. Tactics like evasion and avoidance only serve to anchor fear more firmly in your mind, for the true test comes in a situation where you have no space to use your usual tactics. Thus, when you discover that you do not have the mental fortitude to endure and dominate the difficulty, you will discover that your fear will grow larger, overcome you and then become your prison.

6

Just as regular gym usage develops physical muscles, so does regular problem solving – not avoidance or disguising – develop mental muscles. Face your challenge. Handle it. Choose to be free. When the bar is set higher than where it used to be, you have to go back a little farther than where you used to stand in order to successfully jump over it. There is no shame in doing what you need to do and going back to basics in order to regroup to achieve a higher goal. If you fall down, you will get up. There is nothing new under the sun. You can handle it!

Understand this: Deal with this challenge, once and for all. Destroy the foundations of fear before it becomes your cage. Do what you have to do to solve your own problems.

�֍

Why do the preflight instructions say: "Put the oxygen mask on yourself before attempting to put it on another"?

I have observed that majority of – motivational speakers, personal coaches, celebrities, business executives, philosophers, religious leaders and spiritual teachers – those who urge us to a life of simplicity, love and generosity do so from their nests of comfort. More often than not, we are the beneficiaries of their experiences *after* they have achieved prosperity as wealth, success or fame. One can easily come away from their teachings with the idea that we should not bother to strive for material things because we will ultimately find no joy in them.

Hogwash.

One thing that has become clear on in this issue is this: It is a lot easier to do good when you have something to give than when you have nothing to give.

Yes, I know some people would point us to the Biblical story of the widow's mite, who dropped her last two coins into the synagogue offering box – but she did have those two coins to give, didn't she? Would she have dropped anything in there had she had absolutely no coins? No. Granted that she chose to give 100% of what she had, she still had to have had the coins to give. Point is, we have to have in order to give.

We have to get before we can give. Even if it is not monetary, we still have to get and keep a healthy mind and body before we can give of ourselves in any relationship with others. We have to know love, be love, experience love, before we can be loving to someone else.

Running on 'Empty' yields emptiness.

Understand this: Again, the preflight instructions say: "Put the oxygen mask on yourself before attempting to put it on another." Acquire, be in a position to give, so that you can actually give.

❈

A challenging lesson that those of us with huge egos find difficult to pass is that of engaging in conflict in a way that makes reconciliation possible. Granted that there are certain situations that really require spectacular bridge-burning outcomes, I daresay that the majority of the conflicts we engage in do not call for these.

An older friend once said to me, "When you quarrel with someone, leave room for reconciliation." This does not mean that reconciliation should be made with an eye to (ab)using the other party or their resources in the future. Reconciliation, as appropriate, should be made in order to recreate the relationship on the basis of respect, understanding and compassion.

Authentic reconciliation, I believe, is a reconnection of equals regardless of age, gender, class, education or any other status.

What does it take to engage in conflict with the possibility of reconciliation? The knowledge that

a. No condition is permanent;
b. People can and do change;
c. The good in the other person outweighs (what we perceive as) the bad;
d. The stress of maintaining the conflict is tremendous and debilitating;
e. Ultimately, the conflicting parties are willing to reconnect with each other.

It takes courage to buck public opinion to do the right thing. Joseph already intended in his heart to put Mary away in private when he found out that she was pregnant before they ever lived together. His culture allowed for him to publicly expose and humiliate her, as well as having her stoned to death for (her supposed) infidelity. Yes, he would have been in the 'right', but at what profit to him? Thank goodness that he overcame that conflict, reconciled himself to the situation, and generations now bless him for it.

There are incidents and memories that will remind us that we haven't quite forgotten and that we haven't quite forgiven. We need to be strong enough to admit and accept this, because forgiveness isn't like making a goal shot; it's more like peeling an onion over time. There is no guilt in taking our time to process our thoughts and feelings... and we shouldn't let anyone (including ourselves) tell us otherwise.

Understand this: Open-mindedness. Understanding. Compassion. Mercy. Reconciliation. Difficult to practice, yet the humane way to live. Even as friends, family and associates say to us, "I would never forgive/accept/tolerate/overlook/&c that!" the decision to reconcile (not to be stupid, victimized, but human) still rests with us, because we know that no one – even ourselves – have ever met the standard for utter perfection.

✕

Determining Our Best Fit

In order to determine our best fit in any relationship or situation, we must know ourselves. We must know what we *need*, not just what we want. Knowing what we *need*, we can observe – with realistic eyes – at what faces us. We can ask the right questions (Will this person or group actually give me what I need? If yes, for how long?) – then make the decision that is right for us.

There is nothing right or wrong about knowing how we are 'wired' and what motivates us. Don't let anyone convince you otherwise! Each one of us is unique; therefore, our tastes and needs are unique as well. Even our uniqueness changes over time! There is no one solution for all questions. There is no guarantee that what has worked for one will work for another.

It takes time to know what we really truly want: the time to know ourselves, to understand ourselves and to accept ourselves as we change with experience. It takes courage to see and know a person or group for what it truly has to offer us, given the track record or other hard evidence. It takes courage to walk away from unhappiness. It takes courage to embrace happiness.

Understand this: Knowing that one day we will die, does it make sense to spend our lives and love on people who only offer what we do not want?

An eagle that lives with chicken, is married to chicken, works with chicken or is befriended or bedeviled by chicken is still not a chicken. Instead, this eagle is faced with two choices, really: take courage and fly away to other eagles, or lose hope, live and die with the chicken.

There are eagles that imagine that they are chickens, just because the 'chicken life' is all that they know. With the chickens, these eagles scratch around in the dirt for scraps of food. Because the chickens don't really fly, these eagles don't know or forget that they can soar high into the skies, to altitudes that are beyond the imagination of chickens. At these elevations, eagles can look directly into the sun, maneuver themselves in the high winds, and survey the earth before deciding where to swoop and what to carry away with their powerful talons. Their nests are in crags high in the mountains, where lesser creatures cannot disturb their young.

An eagle that continues to live like a chicken may eventually find that it's fate becomes like that of the chicken – destined for the cook's pot. It will be slaughtered, plucked, quartered, cooked and eaten by those who eat chickens.

Understand this: If you know that you are an eagle, but are not living like one, take a moment now to consider why, then decide how to get out of the chicken coop. You serve no one, most of all yourself, no good where you are now. You deserve better.

✖

The Prodigal Son's Formula

The prodigal son, according to the Bible, was the immoral son who forced his father to cough up the son's share of his inheritance before his death. As the tale went, this incorrigible fellow squandered his fortune and ended up living and feeding swine. Of course, in the Jewish culture, contact with swine was very non-kosher. It was defiling to the Jew and against God's commandments.

After a while of living like this, this son pondered his situation, and finally convinced himself that he could go home to his father. His plan was to return to his father's house, beg for his father's forgiveness, accept any punishment meted out to him by his father (including the possibility of servitude), and thereafter live a wholesome, kosher life.

This, for me, was the interesting part of this prodigal's story. What was illustrative was that, during this period of filthy living, the young man "*came to his senses*" and started *speaking to himself.* No one else did. He compared where he was with where he could be. He understood that there was a chance of success, no matter how slim. He humbled himself sufficiently enough to make it happen. And as the story went, his return home was greeting with an unexpectedly overwhelming welcome by his father.

Many of us have become settled with our lives of dead-end desperation. We have become hardened to futile existence resulting from poor life decisions. We have not yet taken the time to consider if we can do better; even when we know that we can, we hardly have enough motivation to rouse ourselves from our stupor to do anything about it. We imagine that it is too late, we are too old, no one will rescue us, we will never be forgiven, or any myriad of discouraging excuses we make to ourselves for remaining in the place of shame and non-achievement.

The good news is that some of us, regardless of our current circumstances, will recover. We know what to do, and will do it. We will turn again; go 'home' to confess those old dreams, no matter how far-fetched or improbable. Then to the astonishment of the world, we will live our dreams.

Understand this: This was the formula of the prodigal son: *Realize. Confess. Return. Recover.*

As long as there is breath in you,
As long as there is mental power in you
As long as you can think for yourself,
You can stop cold,
You can turn around,
You can start again,
You can do it over.

People, who are running scared in their own lives, will tell you that it isn't doable. Pointing at the failures, they will tell you that others have tried and failed. They will tell you that only younger people or those with connections can succeed. They will question your credentials for undertaking the work you are doing. They will question your worthiness. They will poke holes in the resources you have at hand for the journey you are intending to undertake. And, even if you have the answers for all their pushbacks, they will still lie to you about your chances for success.

When you get fed up with the storytelling and excuses, you will scuttle the unprofitable relationship that feeds you lies. And then you will discover that you wasted time expecting help from the wrong quarters. Later, after you have grieved over time wasted, you'll gather that it is okay. Then you will set your teeth, bare your claws, put your head down, and go at it. The important thing is to get going where you want to go.

Understand this: It's a barefaced lie that it's too much or too late for you. If you want it, get it.

�֎

"Let me see what phone calls I can make on your behalf," she said to me. "You understand that your job at this corporation is tenuous at best right now. You have stepped on the wrong toes. Believe me, I know that you are telling the truth of what happened to you. But you know that jobs are hard to come by and the money is good. All you had to do was keep your head down, keep your mouth shut and be obedient."

In that one moment I knew that it was time for me to make the break for my freedom, while I still had the energy and determination to do so. I did not want to be like her, *brainwashed, powerless, subservient, de-feminized, with no options, decades later.* So I fled and never looked back.

Trust me, it is rarely to your advantage to be obedient to a paycheck that comes with indignity. Unless you already have an immediate exit strategy – which will better your life – all mapped out and waiting, you do incalculable damage to your psyche when you stay where you're not wanted. The wounds you get here will continue to hurt decades after they were initially inflicted on you.

Is it worth it to you to go through life injured and in pain, and inflicting the same on those near and dear to you?

If you have been let go, asked to leave, or have the opportunity to flee any painful/non-profitable relationship (job, affair, family, business, &c), see it for what it really is: *A Huge Advantage*, not a huge adversity. Yes, you might initially worry about how you'll 'make it' (without the money, status, connection, &c); however, do you realize that you are now free to 'make it' differently in a new way with new people – as you are no longer bound by the laws, opinions and expectations of the old relationship?

Understand this: Ultimately, it's on you. If you have to dance naked in the streets to make it happen, do it. Amaze yourself and your skeptics by doing what you were told would you couldn't afford to do.

�֎

During my college days, one of the greatest shocks I experienced as a new computer training volunteer was to hear a job seeker talk of how she was looking forward to reuniting with her abusive husband after his release from jail.

"I really don't want to get a job, " she confided, "He's a good provider and I *know* [*sic*] he love me and the kids."

She didn't believe me when I told her that she could make an even better living, injury-free, dignity intact.

"I'm just a high school dropout. Who would want me anyway?"

For each example I gave her of those who had made it in life without a college degree, she had an excuse: "They must have come from a rich family!" "They must be smart!" "They don't have an accent!" and the ultimate excuse: "They are lucky!"

The best I could do under the circumstances was to sow the seed in her mind.

Self-worthiness is an internally developed quality. It cannot be 'awarded' or conferred by another. Many of us make the mistake of believing that the approbation of others validates one's self-worth. Nothing is farther than the truth here; if you do not hold your own head high, others will surely put their foot upon your neck.

True, there are occasions of embarrassment about our circumstances or misgivings about our deeds, but these are not any measure of our self-worth. Who doesn't make mistakes? Who is *always* presented in the best of lights? None of us. Therefore, we must remember that the better part of who we are forever triumphs who we appear to be, all the time.

Just a few minutes ago, I was speaking with an older cousin about the possibility of being introduced to a man who was looking for a life partner. Before I could finish describing him to her, she jumped in with, "Oh, he couldn't possibly want someone as short and old as me! *All men* are looking for much younger prettier women to marry!" She, who was well known in our social circles to be the epitome of kindness, compassion and hospitality, was saying this!

The sense of our own self-worth gives us the right to be here. Self-worth is what reminds of what we are here to do. Self-worth reminds us of what we bring to the table. Self-worth is what enables us to make the better – or best – decisions for ourselves. Self-worth is what tells us what not to either tolerate or accept. The knowledge of our own self-worthiness is what preserves, vivifies and encourages us.

Understand this: It's all in how you think about yourself. Self-worth is developed by self-knowledge, self-awareness and self-forgiveness. We cannot value that which we know absolutely nothing about or are unwilling to accept. In order to act with boldness, we must know our own self-worth.

✻

The Power of Story

For each one of us, there is a basic trigger, some personal, sad story that brings on the most debilitating sorrow or pain because of the recall of one or more past hurtful occurrences. More likely than not, with this recall, we go into 'hiding' of one sort of another – indulgence in some addiction, emotional outburst, destructive behavior, glossing over, repressing or whatever we think that will pull us out of the maelstrom of overwhelming feelings. This is natural and expected; the question is: Does this 'hiding' effectively deal with the trigger once and for all? Usually not. We 'hide' again and again. And again.

No amount of wishful thinking can remold the past and make it perfect or right. I think most of us have already figured that part out by now. No amount of vengeful thinking can annihilate the 'enemy', whomever or whatever it was; we also know this. What then remains for us to do is to deal with the experience directly.

We need to get to the point of asking ourselves, "What now?" whenever our sad memories are triggered. "What should I do about this? Will I forever remain helpless in the face of this feeling? How can I accept what happened and move on?" We must keep asking these questions of ourselves until we get the answer that is right for us.

Understand this: Memory is all about the power of the story we tell ourselves. The more we review the memory, the more it embeds itself and increases in power inside our own minds. Just as we have the ability to review and focus on our sad stories, we can do the same with better stories that positively reinterpret our experiences. We can deliberately create good memories and embed them deeply in our minds. The good ones then serve to counteract and diminish the power of the sad ones upon recall. This is how change is effected with the power of the stories we tell ourselves.

Pay attention to what is happening to you right now! This person who you believe is tormenting – or at least bugging! – your life is actually a disguised master teacher. That is what is going on. Forget about focusing on the person, for a minute, and focus on what is actually in progress as you interact with this person. Here's what to focus on, right now:

- What do you need to know?
- What do you need to do?
- Where do you need to go?
- What do you need to say?
- What will set you free from this experience, so that you can move on with your life?

The lesson here is for you to acknowledge what you will and will not accept in your life, and then do something about it to make your choice quite clear. If you don't make your own decision, if you remain fearful of the 'consequences' or stay to 'fight' and prove yourself 'right', the Master Teacher will remain with you – or be replaced by another who will take over your 'classroom' to continue the 'syllabus'.

Understand this: As soon as you get clear on what you want, and act quickly, this master teacher will leave you wiser, more insightful, relieved, happy, grateful and completely unresentful. You will also be excellently equipped to navigate your future environments and opportunities.

❧

In the moment, the thing appears very important and very urgent. Eventually we learn and remember that one thing supersedes another: new relationships replace existing ones, new things take the place of the old, and that which was indispensable becomes outdated. Every situation has a solution, no matter how far-fetched or how unwanted such a solution may be.

We must practice putting things in perspective. That which annoys us now most likely will not matter in 24 to 48 hours from now. Billions before us dealt with the same issue, and billions after us also will, albeit in a different format in a different context.

As I write this as the sun begins its descent, I think of my past relationships, some good, some sour, and some fond. Each relationship rose and set beyond the horizon of daily living. Some set 'forever'; some rose again. In hindsight, I see that each relationship served its function, providing lessons, developing character and creating memories. It is perspective that reminds me that this is how life is always lived, two people – family, friends, foes – interacting with each other.

Understand this: Many a time, it's a tall order to see things in perspective in the heat of the moment, but it is something we must learn to do.

✺

"Are you married?"
"No, I'm not."
"Why not? You are a very beautiful woman. Do you have a problem with men?"
"No, I don't have a problem with men. I choose not to get married, at least for now."
"How can you say you don't want to get married? God said that every woman must marry!"
"Really? When did God tell you that all women must marry?"
"It's written in the Bible! Don't you believe the Bible as God's word?"
"Really? Where exactly is it written in the Bible that God said that all women must get married?"
"I don't know the particular place where it's written, but I know it's in the Bible. Our pastor has said so on more than one occasion."

The majority of misinformation that brings us grief comes from solely depending on the utterances and writings of others. Marketers, advertisers and public relation experts know this from experience and results: Repetition creates the impression of truth. An idea presented frequently enough becomes memorized and accepted as fact by majority of the populace.

The sheer volume of information available right now on just about any topic overwhelms many of us. Moment by moment, even more information is added around the world to what is already available! As a result, we would rather that someone else do the research and tell us what is important, what is true and what to do. But this choice leaves us open to negative manipulation. How do we know that the person is not presenting us with information that inures to their profit at our expense? If and when we eventually find out that this is the case, we complain that we were hoodwinked.

We look for someone to blame and to punish. We look for compensation.

Then we do it all over again.

We do not have to know every thing; we can pick whatever faces us at the moment and spend a little time studying and understanding it to the best of our abilities. We can read up on it. We can focus our study on the basics of it, understanding how the thing works, cutting out the theories and discarding doomsday predictions. Then and only then can we make a decision as to what we will do, if we have to do anything.

The important thing is to know for ourselves! So much is lost when we fail to *read* for ourselves! If you have read and understood something for yourself, how can someone come along and tell you that it's written otherwise? When you *know*, you will not be stuck for a ready answer or appropriate action.

Understand this: The obligation to **know** the truth still lies squarely upon us. We cannot blame anyone but ourselves if it is within our power to find out the truth for ourselves.

✄

"You will never make it without me!"
"I made you what you are today!"
"You can't do anything else."
"You don't know how to do anything else."
"Why play with a guaranteed thing?"
"Why do you want to suffer for nothing?"
"Be satisfied with what you got."
"Be thankful for the little you have."
"Don't be greedy!"
"Without me, you are nothing!"
"You will do as I say, whether you like it or not."
"This is how it is."
"Are you ungrateful?"
"This is not for women/girls/boys/men/black people/white people/&c."

Blah, blah, blah.
Are these statements true?
If you had alternatives, would they (still) be true?

Understand this: When you create alternatives for yourself, other people's meaningless rules and rituals no longer bind you. Armed with options, you discover that you're not a prisoner after all. You can walk away.

�֍

In general, publicly available studies have shown that music can elevate or depress the mood. It is a great influencer, and has been used as such for ages. Music affects the mind – both the conscious and the subconscious parts. Many a message has been delivered and reinforced in the mind via music. That is why despotic leaders and governments feel threatened by musicians and their creative outputs, even to the point of putting the artistes to death.

In many nations outside the United States and Canada, it is not uncommon to hear both women and men hum tunes or burst into song as they go about their daily tasks. This they do openly and unashamedly. It is also culturally accepted in many of these places to sing to another to convey a message they need to understand, or to render praises to their Maker.

How can we use this knowledge to our advantage? Personally, I use music to reinforce certain concepts within my own psyche. To make this happen, I select music with lyrics I can understand and agree with. Then I listen for the tune – is it catchy enough to make me repeat the lyrics? I also select certain lyric-less music for their mood-modulating effects. The gamut runs from classical to neo-soul. Whatever resonates with me at a profound level, whatever harmonies I can individually detect, whatever makes me smile…. that's what I go for.

It is a pity that most of us hear our daily or weekly quota of music via television and radio advertisements, or telephone music when we're put on hold! The most songs that a lot of people remember are the ones from days bygone. What a tragedy! If we were to realize the potency of music, what it can do for us and how freely, we would be very reluctant to continue medicating ourselves with drugs, food, alcohol and other activities that create so much unnecessary mental noise in our heads. We can be soothed, invigorated, inspired, hopeful, spiritual or mellowed by the right choice of music. We can be switched instantaneously from our present environment to another by hearing music that is associated with the memory of the other place.

Understand this: In these days of stress and strain, a quick way to change your mood without side effects is just to listen to pleasant music. Get something to make you dance or sing along. You can start or end your day on a pleasant note (pun intended!) by resetting your brain's centers of sensation with music.

✂

Lots of fun. Piano music in the background. Side tables loaded with various potluck dishes. At various times, we walked over to hug the guest of honor – an elderly man, who lived all by himself, though you couldn't have told it from the number of people in the church dining room. Many of us called him Father, others, Brother; a couple of comely matrons pseudo-squabbled over who was his true ladylove. The rest of us roared with laughter. His face was beet red as he laughed aloud and pleaded for peace.

Then someone started clinking silverware to glass to gain our attention. The room got quiet as we listened; tears of joy began to glisten on many cheeks as he thanked us – of different colors and accents and backgrounds – for being his true family.

Understand this: Your true family is the people you discover yourself; the ones you love because you chose them, and they love you because they chose you.

✺

www.ingramcontent.com/pod-product-compliance
Lightning Source LLC
Chambersburg PA
CBHW060607030426
42337CB00019B/3644